I₁

Published by:
Michigan Writers Cooperative Press
P.O. Box 2355
Traverse City, Michigan 49685

İΠΚ

A Memoir

KATHLEEN PFEIFFER

To Judy
With my fond regards —

Kathleen Pfeiffer

MICHIGAN WRITERS COOPERATIVE PRESS 2018

for Brian
your souvenir

There is nothing you can do except try to write it the way that it was. So you must write each day better than you possibly can and use the sorrow that you have now to make you know how the early sorrow came. And you must always remember the things you believed because if you know them they will be there in the writing and you won't betray them. The writing is the only progress you make.

— Ernest Hemingway, *The Garden of Eden*

⊕NLY +HE G⊕⊕D DIE Y⊕UNG

They showed you a statue and told you to pray
They built you a temple and locked you away
— Billy Joel, *Only the Good Die Young*

A ll of us girls were barefoot — we had kicked off our platform shoes back when "50 Ways to Leave Your Lover" came on. We all wore prairie skirts and flouncy, ruffled tops, like Phoebe Cates in *Seventeen* magazine. We tucked Bonne Belle Kissing Potion into our pockets, and we parted our hair down the middle, with one side tucked back in a tortoise shell comb and the other side flipped with a curling iron, Farrah Fawcett-style.

On a Friday night in June, 1978, we were celebrating our eighth grade graduation at St. Catherine of Siena School in Trumbull, Connecticut, with a boy-girl dance in the church basement. Father Malloy was there to chaperone, and he stood alongside the boys who were too shy to dance. We kept watch on Sister Theresa: during slow songs, we'd heard, she'd take out a ruler to measure the distance between couples. *Leave some room for the Holy Spirit*, we were warned. The floor was dusty beneath our bare feet, and the lights were dimmed.

All of us girls loved to dance, and we owned 45's by Shaun Cassidy and Andy Gibb. We had memorized the lyrics to "Bohemian Rhapsody." Even though my stomach had hurt from nervousness throughout the day, I was happy to be there, dancing. Happiness was such a relief after so many months of uncertainty and fear. I had been practicing the Bus Stop in my basement, replaying the Beach Boys over and over until I got the steps right. I would not be the dork who missed a turn and stepped on someone's foot. I smelled like all my friends: Tickle deodorant and Love's Baby Soft.

Lisa Healy and I were practicing The Bump when "Stayin' Alive" faded out and I first heard those upbeat piano chords that shook me like a tremor. I was afraid this would happen, even though the

DJ was from our church and he should have known better. How could anyone be so stupid? I scanned the room in shocked silence, looking around, while all the other girls squealed with delight. They loved this song, brand new Billy Joel, and everybody sang along, shouting the lyrics they already knew by heart.

Only the good die young? My little brother's grave was so fresh that the grass seed probably hadn't even sprouted above him yet. This was not what I wanted to be reminded about at my school dance.

I left the floor. Grabbing my shoes from the pile, I slipped my feet in, and ran to the door, wondering if anyone would notice me leaving. I wanted someone to see me. I wanted someone to follow.

Here's what I remember: Gerry was a goofy kid, with crooked front teeth, oversized eyeglasses, and wavy, flyaway hair. He was eleven the year he died, younger than me by two years and two months, but he was the oldest boy, so he had a status in the family that I couldn't ever hope to achieve. According to family rumor, Grandpa was so thrilled to have a grandson, finally, after the three of us girls, that upon hearing of Gerry's birth, he kept repeating, "You're sure it's a boy?" Gerry got to be an altar boy in all of its cassocked glory. I was so jealous; before Mass, he had backstage access to the warren of cubbies and closets behind the altar, and after Mass, he got to play basketball with Father Malloy. Gerry once confessed to me that he'd tasted the communion wine but the flavor of alcohol was too strong and it scared him. This didn't surprise me. He was a scaredy cat, even afraid of swimming under water. I would taunt him, singing:

Ask any mermaid you happen to see,
What's Gerry Pfeiffer? Chicken of the Sea!

He was afraid of the dentist and he hated needles. Once I sat in Dr. Rogalewski's waiting room and listened to Gerry scream at the Novocain injection, a tortured howl of pain. That made me hate our dentist, made me want to run back there and punch him.

Gerry was always skinny, and he loved tomato sandwiches, with a thick slathering of mayonnaise. I hated tomato sandwiches, and I especially hated mayonnaise, but Mom served them all the time, it seemed, because they were *his* favorite. He never crumbled Ritz crackers in his chicken noodle soup the way Marianne and Susan and I did, instead keeping them in a neat pile beside his bowl to nibble in between spoonfuls. One year, Mom made him a train cake for his birthday, and we weren't allowed in the kitchen all day so we wouldn't distract her. Other years she made him a teddy bear cake with Oreo cookie ears and chocolate dusted coconut fur, and an ocean cake topped with toy boats and frosting fishes.

He was the first of us kids to get glasses and, following our father's lead, we all called him "the professor" once he started wearing them, but we pronounced it *Pro-fessa*. He was named after my father, but we never called him Junior, only Gerry. Sometimes Gerry Junior. When he got in trouble, we'd hear his full name bellowed out throughout the house, but this was true for all of us. Once Paul was born, there were five of us kids and a lot of rules, so there was a lot of getting into trouble.

One day we were in the living room packing up towels and swimsuits for a trip to the indoor pool at the high school, when Gerry stood up quickly with a confused look on his face. "Something just happened," he said to Mom, hand on his abdomen. "Something just pulled inside me, like it broke or something." Turned out he had a hernia, and he was the first of us kids to ever go to the hospital for an operation. Wait, no. He was the only one of us kids to go to the hospital, ever.

Gerry and I were not the closest in age, but it felt like we were, especially at the start of my eighth grade year, when he was starting fifth. That year, Marianne and Susan were both in high school, and so they rode a different bus and went to basketball games on Saturdays. Susan and I had always shared a room, but it had gotten smaller as we grew up; we didn't talk as much anymore, and she was often impatient with me. Paul, still the baby, was in second grade, so Gerry and I got thrown together a lot, sharing chores and bedtimes, supervising Paul as we three walked to school together. Gerry would talk to me about his classes as we walked, about his shyness, and about how he wished he was better at basketball. I told him about my crushes and swore him to secrecy. That was the year we started speaking to each other in baby talk, especially when we wanted to be serious. "I wuv woo," I'd call to him at night from my bedroom down the hall.

✝

Gerry had his first seizure in October, 1977. I was sitting in English class, daydreaming, when Mrs. DiLalla stuck her head in my classroom door. She was my friend Nancy's mother, the school secretary; everybody knew everybody at St. Catherine's. It was early, before lunch.

"Kathy Pfeiffer?" she called. "We need you down at the office, Hon."

Out in the hall, she patted my back and leaned in.

"Gerry's got a stomach ache, sweetie," she explained. "Can you go into Miss Z's cloak room and get his things? Your mother's here to take him home. That's a good girl."

As I carried his coat and lunch box down the hall to the nurse's office, I practiced baby talking, thinking of something to say that might cheer him up. "How's my widdle bwudder?" But I was stopped at the door, and the nurse wouldn't let me in. Mom was in there, but so was Father Malloy with his EMT equipment. Gerry lay on the cot, motionless and pale. Mom was leaning forward, speaking to him in a low voice when she heard me at the door and turned.

"Thanks, Kath!" she called out. "We've got this covered. You can go back to class." She had been a surgical nurse for many years. This was her work voice.

I didn't even know that an ambulance had come until Jimmy O'Neil reported the excitement to our class on his way back from the lavatory. Even then, I didn't connect the ambulance to Gerry because I figured he was already home on the couch, watching TV. A few minutes later, Sister Theresa walked in. Her tall, thin frame always leaned slightly forward, her head bowed in the manner of a Virgin Mary statue. As usual, we all stood up while the principal was in the room.

"Good mawning class," she nodded at us, speaking with the careful enunciation of an English teacher and with the dropped r's of a Dorchester native. "I know that some of you sore an ambulance in the pahking lawt and I want you to know there's nothing to be worried about. Little Gerry Pfeiffer from the fifth grade was having some trouble and we called the paramedics as a preecawshun. At times like these, it's very impawtant not to gawsup." She turned to look Jimmy O'Neil straight in the eye for a long beat, and then she continued. "I know that we all will keep Gerry and his family in owuh prayuhs."

Thirty pairs of eyes turned toward me and stared. My head swirled black, and I grasped the side of my desk. Sister nodded and left the room. We all sat back down and said the Our Father together, me joining in with the class as if it wasn't even my own brother we were praying for, but some anonymous child from UNICEF.

✝

Years later, when I was in college, my father visited Boston for a convention and he took me out to dinner. That night, I first learned all the details of Gerry's disease and prognosis. He had had a seizure that day in October. He had several more in the weeks following. The doctors discovered pretty quickly that a brain tumor was causing his seizures and in January, at the time of his surgery, the projection was grim. They gave him six, maybe nine months following the operation; he only lived another three.

"Wait, you knew he was going to die? Why didn't you tell us?"

"Tell you? And have all you kids just moping around, waiting for him to die? We didn't want his last days to be like that. It was so — " he paused, looking for the right word. "Traumatic. It was all just so traumatic. We did the best we could."

Gerry was in the hospital often during those six and a half months between his first seizure and his last. When he was home, he was infirm, either camped out on a sofa in front of the TV, or propped up in bed. I would visit him after school and tell him about my day, pass along school gossip, and sing. *You are my sunshine, my only sunshine. You make me happy when skies are gray.* When he was in the hospital, I visited as often as I could, but it was never as often as I wanted. I brought a notebook and tried to copy down the information from his medical charts; I wanted to know what was happening, I wanted to understand. The medical terminology was beyond me, however, and my mother claimed that it was too technical for her to explain when I asked.

Ours was a small-town Catholic-family parish, and when everyone learned that Gerry was sick, our tragedy became a community event. His seizures took place behind the curtained windows of my parents' neat colonial home, and all the messiness of his vomit and screaming, all of Mom and Dad's frantic calls to 911, all of our anxious, hushed hiding out in our bedrooms — all of this was hidden behind our house's trim exterior, the white paint, the pine green shutters, the symmetrical linden trees and potted chrysanthemums flanking our front door. But when the ambulance came screaming down our quiet street, neighbors could surely hear. People knew. One afternoon, I was talking to Katie Helfrich on the phone when Dad picked up another extension and interrupted our call, his voice shaking. "Whoever it is on the phone you have to *please* hang up *now. Please.* We need an ambulance." I didn't even say goodbye to Katie — I just hung up. A few hours later, Mrs. Helfrich delivered a pan of lasagna to our house, still warm from her oven.

We were showered with food: chicken divan, macaroni casseroles, crockpot beef stews, tomato soup cake, frosted walnut brownies. The feast was a bounty like nothing we'd ever had before, completely unlike Mom's prudent, bland meals. When Gerry was in the hospital, I was often queasy. For much of that winter, I was never hungry. And yet, when the food arrived, I ate everything.

Each of his hospital admissions inspired religious classroom projects at school. As his older sister, I would be presented with the dozens and dozens of handmade "Get Well" cards and posters and prayer booklets produced by the younger children, so I could deliver them to him. For each hospital stay, those faith-filled pictures decorated his hospital room walls. *Put Your Faith in God!* the third graders counseled him, their words embellished with Crayola rainbows and tissue paper roses.

Before Gerry got sick, my life had been going great. Eighth grade was a big year: confirmation, graduation, boy-girl parties, softball. I had watched as Marianne and Susan had taken their turns in the spotlight and I was ready.

"How would you like your own room?" Mom had asked me over Saturday morning pancakes at the start of the school year.

"Seriously?" I squealed. "YES! Yesyesyes!"

"Now that Susan's in high school, I was thinking we could move you into the attic," she explained. "As long as you don't mind those horrible blue walls. We can get you some new wallpaper eventually. And it's going to be colder than your room now."

"Oh, it's not going to be the attic any more," I declared, giddy with excitement, and brushing past any drawbacks. "It's going to be the penthouse!"

That weekend I moved into the empty, uninsulated room on our third floor. I had always wanted a room of my own, so I didn't mind that the rusty steam radiator made creaking noises every time the heat kicked on, or that I had to shiver through an unheated hallway and staircase to walk between my penthouse and the second-floor landing below. I had the whole floor to myself, the attic and all of its treasures: our Christmas ornaments, Mom's prom dresses that we used for dress-up, the *Funk & Wagnalls* encyclopedias, our doll cradle and the doll's dish cabinet with its miniature Blue Willow china. All of our books were up there, Nancy Drew and Cherry Ames and the Dana Girls, the *Little House* series, along with *Little Women, Little Men,* and *Jo's Boys.*

I loved my penthouse, loved the solitude, the privacy. I was Jo March, hiding up in her garret with a stack of books and a fountain pen, her nose smudged with ink. I plotted stories and kept a secret journal. I always pressed hard on ballpoint pens so that my fingers would be stained blue. I wiped my face often, hoping to leave a splotch. When Gerry got sick, I decided that he was my Beth, and I started writing about him. I conducted a bedside interview while he was in the hospital and worked the details of his brain surgery into a feature story for the January edition of our school newspaper. Gerry told me more about the procedure than my parents ever had. He answered my questions in a calm, quiet voice, explaining how they would slice his skull open in a horseshoe shape and peel back the layers to get at the brain tissue. I submitted my typewritten account to Mrs. Marusa. She returned the pages to me unmarked, explaining gently that she felt my story would be too upsetting for the younger students to read.

"But we don't have to give it to them," I suggested. "We could just pass it around to the upper classes."

"It's a beautiful story," she said. "I just think it's too personal."

"But Gerry said it was okay. He wanted people to know."

She shook her head no, smiling gently. That was that.

You got a nice white dress and a party on your con-fir-ma-tion. Billy Joel's lyrics seemed to speak to me directly. My Holy Confirmation took place on a Friday evening, April 28. I wore a dress of pale blue cotton lawn, homemade from a Butterick See & Sew pattern. Soft and blousy, it had a square collar trimmed in white eyelet lace. Grandma finished it at the last minute, sewing the sash and stitching my hem because mom was at the hospital all day.

Until that morning, Gerry had been doing exceptionally well. During the three months following his surgery, the scar was healing, he was tolerating the radiation treatments, and he had even been able to attend Mass a few times. Mom and Dad had arranged for his favorite nurse from the pediatric ICU to stay with him at the house while we all went to church for my Confirmation Mass. We were ready for a great day. But Gerry's screaming woke me that morning. I hid in my bed, alone in my attic room, quakey and scared. By then, I knew well enough to stay out of the way. I peered sideways out my window when I heard the clatter of paramedics leaving the house, and watched from behind a ruffled pink curtain as the gurney slid my brother's small body into an ambulance.

Later that morning, Mom called from the hospital.

"Kath, Honey," she began, in a voice more tender than I'd ever heard before, "I can't leave here. I'm sorry, but I just can't. Father Malloy says that if you want to, you can wait and make your confirmation with the Saint Theresa's eighth grade class in two weeks. It's your choice."

"Two weeks?" I repeated. "But what about Saint Catherine's?" I paused, thinking about those stupid Saint Theresa's girls on our rival softball team. They always beat us. "I hate Saint Theresa's."

"I know," she sighed. "Well, you can keep with the plan for tonight, but I won't be able to be there. Maybe not Daddy, either. I'm sorry, but we just can't leave here."

"When can I come visit?"

I wanted to see him. I wanted to sing him "You Are My Sunshine" like I had when he was home.

"I don't know, Honey," her voice shook. "It's not going well. This is not a good time."

I had been looking forward to my Confirmation day for a full year, ever since I had heard the Bishop tell Susan's Confirmation class that they would feel the love of Christ burning in their hearts at the moment he anointed their foreheads with oil. I believed him literally. I wanted to feel that warmth, to experience the Holy Spirit as a physical sensation. Then I would be ready for adulthood, and I would know, from the burning in my heart, that God loved me in particular. But when we got to church, I was constantly distracted, because I kept turning around to see if my parents had arrived. Uncle Butch, my godfather, was my sponsor and he sat beside me whispering jokes during the homily. In the moment when the Bishop anointed my forehead with warm oil, I felt Uncle Butch standing behind me, solid and kind. "I'm proud of you," he murmured as we walked back to our pew, his hand holding steady between my shoulder blades, now slouched in disappointment. My heart wasn't burning, and I felt the same as before.

Over the next three days, my grandparents came to stay at the house while my parents were at Gerry's bedside. I kept asking to go to the hospital, but there was never a good time. With every phone call, I asked again.

"No, he's still unconscious," Mom explained. "He can't talk to you. It would be too upsetting."

"Well, but maybe he can *hear* me," I protested. "And why does Susan get to go? Why not me?"

"She's older."

"One year! She's one year older than me! Why does that make a difference?"

Grandma took the phone away and scolded me. I never went to the hospital that weekend. Mom and Dad came home together on Monday night right after *M*A*S*H* ended and told us that Gerry was dead.

Then it was too late to see him, or to talk, or to sing to him, or to say goodbye. In all those weeks, even after all those seizures, after his surgery, after the radiation treatments, after all the ambulance calls, the thought had never once occurred to me that he might actually die.

But Virginia they didn't give you quite enough in-for-ma-tion. Mom and Dad didn't see any reason for us to stay home, so the next morning we went to school as usual. Paul and I stood fidgeting in the hallway during the St. Catherine's morning prayer and listened as Sister Theresa explained very gently about how God had picked a flower to make heaven more beautiful. I moved in a fog that day, unsure how to respond when so many people came up to me saying how sorry they were, so I comforted them. Sometimes, if it was a younger student, I would try to joke. I didn't cry at all that day. The next evening, at his wake, Father Paul offered the homily and explained what a thoughtful boy Gerry was, that the last thing Gerry had said before he fell into a coma at the hospital was to ask about me, Kathy, to worry about my Confirmation. "He didn't want to ruin his sister's special day," Father Paul explained, as a murmur spread through the funeral parlor.

Stunned, I felt my chest crack open and I sobbed myself breathless. Gerry was asking for me and I didn't know? They wouldn't let me go see him? Father Paul's homily broke my heart, and the brokenness unfurled into a future in which my brother was dead, and would always be dead, always watching over me from the heaven where he'd been planted like a flower to beautify the hereafter. I wondered if from his cloudy perch he could hear my thoughts and watch what I was doing. I remembered the ceiling at our childhood church, St. Boniface, where God and Jesus and all the saints were lounging overhead, reclining on all the clouds in heaven, watching everything we did down below.

And if Gerry could die like that, so fast, no warning, then who was safe? Who would go next? I saw the rest of my life as a waiting game, to be spent wondering when the next catastrophe would hit.

Afterwards, the unspoken rule in my family was that we did not say his name. We never talked about what happened, not even once, and we never mentioned death, or the hospital, and we never once visited the cemetery together. Once, only once, I tried to talk about my grief.

"I think I've learned an important lesson from all this," I told my mother when we were alone in the car on a grocery trip. "When you cry yourself to sleep a lot, your ears get really wet."

I was trying to tell her how sad I was. I was asking for help. I wanted to explain all the things inside me that I couldn't understand. I wanted to know how she felt, what she did with all her sadness.

"Tears in your ears!" she exclaimed with a laugh.

"Yes."

"That was a song from before you were born," she explained. "Homer and Jethro. *I've got tears in my ears from lyin' on my back in my bed while I cry over you.*"

She sang it with a twang, chuckling. I understood that I should change the subject.

A few days after the funeral, I had come home to discover that Gerry's bed was gone and his clothes had been packed away. The hospital remnants disappeared too — the Pepto-Bismol, the barf bucket, the mattress pad, the plastic water jugs, all the miniature bottles of Keri lotion, which we would rub into his perpetually dry skin — all that got tossed into the trash. Still, there was so much left that could never be discarded. Letters, notes, Mass cards, mementos, his Bible, his stuffed Fleegle Frog, his scapular, the St. Christopher medal, his baby book, and all those messages and cards and drawings from the children at our school.

My mother packed these artifacts into an old green trunk and hauled the collection up to the attic. It rested beside the doll's china cabinet at the top of the stairs, and I passed by that trunk daily. I saw Gerry all the time, said good morning and good night, tapped on the green painted wood for good luck. That trunk may as well have been his casket. I knew that miles away, in the Gates of Heaven Cemetery, his small, encoffined body was quietly decomposing, buried and hidden from view, and settling into the dark earth beneath the verdant landscape.

There, however, at the top of the creaky wooden stairs, I also knew that the remnants of his interrupted life remained behind. Late at night, while my family slept below, I would sit up alone, reading through those sweet, innocent pages and quietly crying. Did the third graders understand what they were making? I imagined them at their desks sharing pots of glue and crayon stubs, imagined my brother floating above me in the sky, invisibly watching everything.

Then, when I couldn't cry anymore, I wrote letters to Gerry on my Postalettes fruit-and-flowers stationary and left them open on my desk, with a blank page and a pen nearby so he could write me back while I slept. Jesus said that if I had faith the size of a mustard seed, then I could move a mountain. I would pray to Gerry each night and ask him to leave me something: a mark, a smudge, anything — I didn't even want a big miracle like in the Bible. I just needed some sign back then — I needed it badly — some evidence that he had existed, and that our awkward sibling intimacy was more than a figment of my imagination. By the end of the summer, I couldn't even remember the sound of his voice, and that felt like a terrible betrayal. I needed *something*, anything besides the looming bully of his absence. My own remembering was too isolated and my recall was dimming; memory alone wasn't enough. I was no longer sure that he was in heaven, watching me, or that he knew I loved him, that I remembered him. I left blank pages for him to mark because I wanted proof, and I wanted it in ink.

GH⊕S✝S

What we remember from childhood we remember forever —
permanent ghosts, stamped, imprinted, eternally seen.
— Cynthia Ozick, "The Shock of Teapots"

Three years later, I was a junior at St. Joseph High School, when a tall, thin boy joined the study hall table where I was sitting with a few friends. He wore the uniform of a sophomore, and I had never seen him before.

"Hi, Jon," someone said.

He grunted, and began thumbing through a dog-eared paperback of Camus's *The Stranger*. We were talking about music when he looked up and joined the conversation.

"Billy Joel?" he scoffed at the mention of *Songs in the Attic*. "What a hack. Remember that song, 'Only the Good Die Young?'" he looked around the table, puffing his cheeks out to spurt air through his pursed lips like we'd been taught in French class. *Ppppfffftt.* "Total crap."

Everyone laughed.

I looked across the table and took him in: the wire-rimmed aviator-style eyeglasses, the smooth, clear skin stretched tight over sharp cheekbones and jaw. The shock of straw-colored hair falling over his forehead, the stiff torso, erect posture, the bitter laugh. He was cute. I leaned forward and tapped his book as the conversation continued around us.

"I hate that song," I said.

Billy Joel's tune had haunted me during the previous years, catching me at unexpected moments and making me shiver. The quaky tremor I'd feel at hearing the opening bars had not dissipated, not in the summer after Gerry died when Mom and Dad told us that Mom was pregnant; not in October when James was born, a year after Gerry's first seizure; not ever. Even as we all found joy again, delighting in James's silly sweetness, that song continued to assault me with all the force it had brought on the night of my eighth grade dance.

"People say that like it's supposed to make you feel better," Jon said, to no one in particular. "It's ridiculous. That's all anybody could say to me at my brother's funeral. It's stupid."

Off in the distance, a bell rang to signal the change of classes.

"Wait," I looked at him, startled. "Your brother died, too?"

It wasn't until many years later that I learned all the details of Jon's loss. His brother, Richard Jr, the firstborn son like Gerry, and also named after their father, was nine years older than Jon. Richard's death took place a year before Gerry's, in a freak accident while pursuing university field work. He was researching his Dartmouth senior thesis in a remote area of Nova Scotia, traveling in the company of a graduate student. Both plunged to their deaths. The drop was 160 feet from a steep incline of rock that proved far more dangerous than it appeared. "It was hazardous in its innocence," commented their supervising professor, after he visited the scene. Their bodies were not discovered until about three weeks after the fall. The youngest of four — now three — sons, Jon was the only child still living at home. By sophomore year, he was suffocating under his parents' constant worry, their relentless prayers, their overbearing attention.

Jon and I traded phone numbers that day in study hall, and for the next few weeks, we talked on the phone whenever possible; although, in my house with five kids and one phone line, both privacy and telephone access were rare. I discovered that he went to St. Catherine's Church for the early Mass, and I quit sleeping in on Sundays so I could see him there.

We left notes in each other's lockers, exchanging thoughts about the world and our fraught complaints about parents who didn't understand us. We read *Jonathan Livingston Seagull* together. He started calling himself Fletch, after the apprentice bird, and he called me Jonathan, like the enlightened teacher gull. Even though

I was a year ahead of him, I couldn't imagine what I might possibly teach him.

I copied out quotes from other Richard Bach books, and we agreed they were really profound. I came across a line that seemed to answer the riddle of Gerry's death, and I inked the words on an index card and slipped the note through the vent of Jon's locker: *Here is a test to find whether your mission on earth is finished: If you're alive, it isn't.* We spent hours pondering over our life's mission. Why were *we* still alive? Why weren't *we* the ones who had died?

Marianne and Susan were boy crazy in high school, and both nursed crushes on basketball players who didn't even know their names. Jon and I were different, I believed. We were philosophical and mature: our friendship existed on a completely different plane than most boy-girl high school relationships. Occasionally, however, he would disappear, avoid my calls, and leave my notes unanswered. "Don't do that!" I'd plead, histrionic, when he finally answered the phone.

"Do what?" he'd ask, nonplussed.

"Disappear. Don't disappear."

"Take a chill pill. I'm not going anywhere. You worry too much."

But he was going somewhere, and he let me know it. He told me he'd started drinking, and he spent many evenings in his basement, lifting weights. I knew he had a bottle of vodka hidden down there, too. Sometimes at school, he'd walk right past me and not even look, not even say hello.

"Dump him," my friend Laura advised, when I shared my worry. "That's bad news."

"No, you don't understand," I insisted. "It's a cry for help. He needs me." I knew that Laura couldn't get it. She'd never had anyone die on her.

During Christmas break, Jon and I would talk on the phone nearly every night, late into the night, after everyone in both of our houses was asleep. Sometimes we'd just stay quiet together and not say anything. I'd turn out all the lights except for the Christmas tree and lie on the floor, squinting up at the blue bulbs. On many nights, the snow fell as we talked, and the silence outside would be soft and deep and comforting. We talked about Christmas last year, before we met. I tried to track where I'd been four years earlier, during Richard's funeral, and I asked where he was in 1978 on May 1, the day Gerry died. *Your friends will know you better in the first minute you meet,* Richard Bach had written, *than your acquaintances will know you in a thousand years.* After staying up so late at night, thrumming with emotion, I'd have trouble sleeping.

I became haunted by dreams. Gerry was out there, somewhere. He wasn't dead at all. I'd catch a glimpse of him, or of someone who I thought might be him, and I'd follow, always at a distance, always missing him before he went around a corner and disappeared. His figure was ahead of me in a dark passageway, a tunnel, and I chased after him, following as he turned a corner and led me into a shadowy cave, curved with a smooth dome overhead. His casket lay against a far wall, dimly lit, flanked at either end by bright floral sprays in yellow and white. Giant chrysanthemums, like the corsages worn by cheerleaders at our Thanksgiving football game.

The casket was always empty.

Or Gerry would be at the mall, and I could pick him out of the crowd, so I'd leave my group of friends, jubilant that I'd found him again, that he was finally within reach. I'd call after him, and he'd look back and see me and wave, but he'd be on the escalator far ahead of me, far above me, and by the time I got to the top, he'd be gone, disappeared into the crowd.

I never thought to wonder if it was actually Jon I was chasing.

✝

Jon understood me. I needed to believe he understood. I needed Jon to be an endless well of understanding, because talking to him gave me a place where I could finally pour out my own sadness and longing and despair. Some days I didn't mind that he ignored me in school, because I knew in my heart that we had a special connection, and I didn't need our friendship to be public in order for his feelings to be real. Other days, I minded, and felt even more lonely, more odd, more separate from my friends, from everyone.

Even on the bad days, I was immensely proud of our friendship. Laura said she thought I just had a crush on him, that I'd get over it eventually. I fretted over this, and comforted myself by thinking that another girl my age simply couldn't understand this kind of friend.

"Laura thinks I've got a crush on you, you know," I said one night on the phone, biting off the dead skin beside my thumb nail.

"I know," he answered. "It's pretty obvious."

My thumb started to bleed. I rubbed the sore spot against my teeth and waited for him to say more.

"Well?" I asked.

"Well what?" he answered. "What do you want me to say?"

"Well, I just don't want things to be weird between us," I explained in a rush. "I mean, I know this is my thing, and I don't have any expectations from you, but I just wanted to say it. I don't want it to screw up the friendship."

"Oh, it's not gonna screw up the friendship," he laughed. "It's cool. I mean, you know I love you, but just not like that."

I exhaled, trembling. He loved me. Only Gerry had ever said that to me before.

In religion class Sister Peter assigned a journal and encouraged us to write down whatever was on our minds, so I wrote about Gerry on every page. I explained that I never got to say goodbye, and I didn't even realize he was going to die until it was too late. I wrote about my Confirmation night, when I couldn't feel the love of Christ burning in my heart, and I was afraid I had done something wrong to keep from feeling it. I confessed how haunted I was by the green trunk that greeted me every night at the top of my penthouse stairs. My word count doubled what the assignment asked for, as my cramped handwriting bled into the margins of my notebook, onto its covers. I waited anxiously for Sister Peter's response. "Thanks for sharing," she wrote in red ink. "B+." I sneaked a look across the aisle and saw the response she wrote in another kids' journal: "Thank you for sharing." I slumped in my chair.

I registered for a spring semester poetry class, thinking that poetry would help me work through my feelings and memories. I was, however, the only student who signed up for the class, so Mrs. Green offered to teach me poetry as an independent study. When she asked which books spoke to me, I mentioned *Jonathan Livingston Seagull*. She nodded. "What about poets?" she asked. I told her about the stack of James Kavanaugh books I'd been collecting from the Hallmark store.

"James Kavanaugh?" she asked. "I don't think I've heard of him."

I mentioned some titles — *Winter Has Lasted Too Long* and *There Are Men Too Gentle to Live Among Wolves*. Many of the poems were iambic pentameter and easy to memorize, so I recited a few lines to show her what interested me. "Gray branches are staring at me, erasing the memory of spring," I chanted. "And we have forgotten the song a hummingbird taught us to sing."

"Okay," she said, nodding. "Those are some lovely images. Let's do an opening unit on nature. How about we start with Richard Wilbur's poem 'The Event'?"

Poetry class was harder than I expected. I wanted to write about my *feelings*, and read work that gave me secret messages like those I found in Richard Bach. But Mrs. Green had me reading Robert Browning, Theodore Roethke, Sylvia Plath. I couldn't understand what they were up to. Sometimes a line or phrase would hook into my brain and haunt me, but I was unable to articulate what made the words resonate for me. When Mrs. Green asked me to scan lines and comment on a poem's structure, I got the meter all wrong. The language was just so cryptic.

✝

Sometimes, as high school went on, I would go a whole day with-out thinking about Gerry, and sometimes, that felt like a relief rather than a betrayal of his memory. By senior year, I was the only Pfeiffer in St. Joe's — Marianne and Susan were away at college, and Paul was still at St. Catherine's. I was busy and I was happy. That spring, I visited Boston for a campus tour, and stayed over-night in the dorm with my future roommate. At school, I landed a speaking part in *Hello, Dolly!* and *Hello, Dolly!* led me to Matt. He used to hang out in the piano room after school where we rehearsed the musical numbers. Matt was so easy, so mellow. He carried none of the heaviness that had followed me since Gerry's death, even though his mother had died a few years earlier. His mother! He had a face like Pac-Man — a wide, ready grin, always laughing, always wry. His father had remarried quickly to a young widow with three daughters the same age as Matt and his siblings, and Matt hadn't reacted to the upheaval in his life at all. He'd play the piano until the girls complained and then he'd put on head-phones and listen to Pink Floyd. Their house was never locked and the kitchen was always supplied with better food than anything we had at home. I spent a lot of time there, eating nachos and watching MTV.

Jon, still a junior, mocked Matt and grew sullen, more distant. I continued to wake early on Sundays, so I could see Jon at church each week — his rigid, muscular form always the tallest in the communion line. As spring passed, however, he often avoided eye contact. I would wait for him after church, but he'd slip out another door. He stopped calling, then he stopped taking my calls, and his silence confused me.

Towards the end of the summer we spoke. I offered to treat him to dinner. We'd celebrate my leaving for college, I explained, we'd celebrate his upcoming senior year. I wanted to recapture the friendship of those late nights last winter, so I could leave for college knowing that we were still connected, Fletch and Jonathan. He agreed, and we set a date. He ghosted me — never showed. I watched the driveway out my window for a long time that night before I admitted to myself that I'd been stood up. At first, I turned to Richard Bach for comfort, rereading from my old notebook: *Don't be dismayed at good-byes. A farewell is necessary before you can meet again. And meeting again, after moments or lifetimes, is certain for those who are friends.* But the sentiment felt hollow, and the wording seemed really stupid. I suddenly realized that I didn't want to waste one of my last nights mooning alone at home, so I drove to Matt's house. We played Atari.

☦

I wrote to Jon from college, and he never answered. If I had been home in my penthouse, his absence would have led me to sulky anxiety; I'd have written him long fervent letters. But in Boston I learned quickly that nobody was interested in the sob story about my dead brother, and also that a lot of fun was to be had drinking beer at the Lambda Chi Alpha house. So drink I did, along with my posse of new girlfriends who shared a love for the Go Go's. We locked arms as we walked down Brookline Avenue singing, *This town is our town, yes it is so glamorous. Bet you'd live here if you could and be one of us!*

When my parents encouraged me to find a marketable degree, I resisted. I wanted to read literature. My English professors took me seriously, like Mrs. Green had, and they offered detailed comments on my papers. I made the Dean's List. Encouraged, I read Virginia Woolf, Ernest Hemingway, William Faulkner. I cultivated a haughty disdain for *Jonathan Livingston Seagull.* In American Literature class, I encountered Wallace Stevens, and his complexity made me look back at my high school taste with embarrassment. The summer after my sophomore year would be my last time living at home. I found that I loved Boston too much to leave, even for the summer, and so I lodged in the dorm, supporting myself with a retail job. I read only Henry James all summer, nearly all his fiction, in preparation for my senior thesis on individualism and self-invention. At the time, it seemed like a literary topic, not a personal one.

"Wow, you're ambitious," a stranger commented on the T one day, as I sat with *The Portrait of a Lady* opened before me. "The Master. That's steep."

"Hurts so good," I smiled.

I went to graduate school, where I was the youngest in my cohort. In year two, I encountered *Moby Dick* for the first time. Naive, eager, and insecure, I saw the novel as a catalogue of my ignorance, and I struggled to prepare for the weekly meetings in my advisor's office. I read each page with a dictionary nearby, taking extensive notes as my fingers cramped around my pen from anxiety. Melville's complicated masterpiece documented all the things I didn't yet know about language, ambition, and history; his insights showed me how little I understood about desire, about longing. I wrote down everything I didn't understand, the pages smeared with my ignorance. Difficulty drew me to Melville. I wanted more of it.

BAD PENNY

I began to think it was high time to settle with myself at what
terms I would be willing to engage for the voyage.
— Herman Melville, *Moby Dick*

One Tuesday morning in 2010, I returned to my English Department office and found my phone's red message button lit up. I had just come back from teaching William Carlos Williams in my undergraduate modernism class, and I had an hour before my next session. Across campus, my husband had just left his own office to teach an American Revolution seminar. Tuesday was my day to collect our son from childcare, so when I punched in the security code to access my voicemail, I was expecting to hear Todd with an update about Brian's pickup time. Instead a deep, unfamiliar voice began talking.

"Well, hello there, Professor. Are you really a professor? Well, I guess I'm not surprised. So, I am calling with a blast from your past. Are you ready? Yes, it's me. Jon. What's up?"

I sat in a dazed silence at my desk, staring out the window as I monitored the fluttering heartbeat of my unexpected joy. *Jon?* Giddy, I closed the office door. I replayed the message to listen again and then again. I had not seen him since high school. He sounded as if we'd just spoken a few weeks ago, as if he hadn't ghosted me all those years ago.

I was far too flustered to speak, so I found him on Facebook and sent a private message in response. "What am I to make of this sudden reappearance?" I wrote.

"I'm like a bad penny," he replied. "I'll email you later."

I was surprised by the intensity of joy I felt in hearing his voice. How many times had I imagined this moment in the past? But I hadn't thought about Jon in years, not in decades. Yet he looked me up, he found me. *He* was thinking about *me*? I closed my eyes and traveled backwards through time and memory to call out to my younger self. *He comes back!* I tell her. *He comes back!* Does it help her, does it make a difference?

I checked my email regularly until his reply appeared. *Let's just say that every once in a while I catch a fleeting glimpse of who I really am in this life,* he wrote, *and I'm reminded of those wonderful people who have helped shape my soul. And so I seek them out and let them know in one way or another how important they are to me and that I think of them fondly and with love.*

I phoned back the next day.

Jon had spent the past three decades wandering the country, I learned, flitting from job to job, from woman to woman, drinking, and getting into plenty of bar fights along the way. The stories tumbled out of him: the trip to Tijuana when he and his buddy got a great deal on some gorgeous leather jackets, but when they got caught in the rain on their way to the airport, they discovered the leather had been cured in urine; the friend's wedding reception when he'd discovered that his first wife was cheating on him, so he punched a marble wall in the bathroom and split his knuckles open; his engagement to a Connecticut socialite that was reported in the *New York Times* before they called it quits.

He'd landed in Florida and worked in IT support, which was great money, although he'd rather have more time to make art. He had been sketching a bit, and wanted to sculpt more. He worked at maintaining a lighthearted tone, but I heard what sounded like the weight of defeat in his voice. He was cool and ironic when talking about himself.

He was friendly and warm, however, in asking about me, and his flashes of wry humor seemed genuinely affectionate. Why was I in Michigan? Should he call me doctor or professor? Do students try to bribe me for good grades, how do I like being a mother, do I still go to church? He asked me to phone him again, but I rarely had freedom or privacy to call or to talk for long during the times he was available. More than that, the immediacy of conversation felt far too intimidating. I wanted more control, more time to think through my answers. I didn't trust myself with speech. *Oh, by the way,* he wrote. *I really do love the way you express your thoughts*

- you are quite gifted. Mine must seem very sophomoric, but I am what I have become. More of a computer geek than the writer I had aspired to be. Ah well, you were always better than I anyway. In email and in texting, I could pin him down, hold him captive. How many times had I explained to my students that writing has permanence, that it has an authority we can never find in the spoken word? I printed his messages out and I still have them today — evidence, proof of everything he said.

Jon remembered so much about who I used to be, and I was stunned to think that he had preserved such distinct memories of *me* for all those years, that he could recall so many details even through the haze of all that vodka. After that first call, we were in daily contact — occasional phone calls when I could snatch some free time but mostly email and messaging. I sensed that it was all too much, and I suspected that such intensity was wrong somehow, but I didn't care. I had a chance to revisit the past and make meaning of that loss. Why did he leave me all those years ago, where did he go, *what happened?* I needed to know. I pressed him on these questions, as if the adult still bore responsibility for the child, as if anything he could say now might reach back in time to comfort the pain I felt then. *One of the absolute, concrete memories I have that I know for sure,* he wrote in reply, *was how intimidated and insecure I felt by the end, when you were leaving for college. I don't think I'll ever be able to fully apologize for that.* He had come to imagine that his life experiences were like pennies in a jar, he explained, collections of images and memories that he was saving up for some future moment. Someday, he was certain, their value would be clear and all those penny-thoughts he'd been saving would lead him to his proper destiny. He simply hadn't found that destiny yet.

"*But I know,*" he wrote, trying to explain, "*that love and that 'thing' you and I had (have) is something I'll never really understand — yet it's there.*" I paused on his parenthetical. *Have?* The intimacy pierced me.

Was this a betrayal? I'd written him about my husband often, talked about my stepdaughter and my son, I had been very clear about my contentment, and about my boundaries. I was clear with myself, too: my life was exactly what I wanted and I'd worked hard to get where I was. Still, Jon's return made me inexplicably happy. It cast doubt on everything that I thought had been happiness before. I carried the secret knowledge of his return with me everywhere — to the grocery store, on the treadmill, in student conferences — as if I had E.T. hidden away in my closet, my own special treasure.

I talked it all through with Todd, hoping he could anchor me back in my real life. Todd had known about Jon from the beginning, and he treated my confusion with gentle compassion.

"Well, he knows you're married, right?" he asked.

"Yeah, that was, like, the first thing I told him," I explained.

"I don't know, Kath," he replied, "that was a hard time for you, and you're still not really over your brother. Remember how scared you got when Brian was born? Maybe it's still hard for him too. Maybe he just really needs a friend right now."

"He sounds really lost."

"You'll figure it out."

I read through my high school yearbook and poked around the old letters and cards in my college trunk, looking to reconstruct the story I'd told myself about those days. The mementos were all there — all the ink-smeared pages we passed back and forth that winter. Jon signed all his letters "Fletch," with a line drawing of two seagulls flying across the horizon, elegant smears of blue along the page. The memories all came back, the gravity of carrying adult grief in our awkward teenaged bodies.

✝

"Ok, then, there's something you oughta know about me," Jon told me one night on the phone. "It might be a deal breaker." I had just explained that I was home alone: Brian asleep, Todd teaching night class.

"It's about my ink," he said. I heard his pull on a cigarette.

"Your *ink*?" I asked.

"Yeah," he answered, interrupting his speech with a jagged cough. "I've got a lot of ink. I mean, a lot. I mean, like, skull and crossbones. It would scare you. Pretty heavy stuff." He chuckled. "Red and black flames. Pure evil."

"Wait, you mean like *tattoos?*"

"Yeah," he laughed. "Ink. What did you think I meant?" I heard a rustling sound as he covered the phone to cough again. "Huh. Maybe it's not an English professor kind of thing. I figured you wouldn't understand."

Perhaps Jon sought me out because he was lonely and depressed. He'd recently been through his second divorce, and I wonder if he was imagining how his life might have been different. His conversation sometimes carried the choking terror of someone who's drowning, and I felt as though our renewed friendship was helping him stay afloat, some kind of a buoy. I could tell when he'd been drinking because his thoughts would become woeful, despairing. His misery circled in on itself. Maybe I'll just go out like Nicholas Cage, he said one night, like in *Leaving Las Vegas*. If Richard hadn't died, he said, he would have had a role model, someone to show him how to be a man. He still missed his brother, and still looked for him everywhere.

"You're the one person who really understood me back then," he said.

He never talked about Richard's death, but he must have thought about it. I imagined it. Yes, Richard and his companion would have seen the steep angle of the rock they were traversing, but they could not have known how slick it was. It must have been a beautiful landscape, actually, just after the rain, blanketed with soft, greeny moss. How long did it take them to fall so far? Did one of them reach to save the other? Was it a comfort to not die alone?

I had been reading my old notes from Jon, and they reminded me of how unmoored we both were in childhood, how isolated. Pray for me, we'd ask each other, help me find my way through this. Even in high school, I still felt the crushing disappointment of that first morning when I woke up to find blankness on the page where I'd asked my dead brother to write me back. Even now, I wonder at the sincerity of my faith in those days, my genuine belief that his ghost could leave me a message. The unmarked paper, as I saw it, meant only one of two things: either my faith wasn't strong enough, or Gerry was utterly lost to me. Those mornings, that blank page would fill me with such buzzing emptiness that I would try to fill them myself, try write myself the letters I wished my brother would write. I would sit at my maple desk, head bowed, waiting for the words to come. *Dear Kathy,* — then what? Gerry was so far away from me that I couldn't imagine what he might possibly say. Until I met Jon, and *he* wrote to me, saying all the things I hadn't known I needed to hear.

"Yeah," I answered. "It was such an amazing coincidence, how much we had in common."

"That's not a coincidence. That's something else."

"Like what?"

"I don't know. But something. It meant something."

Six weeks in, I bought a plane ticket to Florida. Ostensibly, I was visiting my Aunt Mickie, and while I had been planning to do that anyway, and I was genuinely glad to spend time with her, my true destination was Jon. I'd fly into the airport closest to him, we'd meet for lunch, and then I'd rent a car to drive the four hours to Mickie's.

"Four hours?" Todd asked. "That's quite a voyage."

"I know," I said. "I know it's crazy. Are you sure you're okay with this?"

"I am if you are," he answered. "I trust you. I just hope you're not getting yourself in too deep."

"I just really feel like we need to talk, like we have this unfinished business that I want to settle. I want to do it in person, in real time."

I told Jon the same thing.

"You know what I'm really looking forward to," I said, one afternoon between classes as Jon was on a cigarette break, "is talking. I really miss talking to you. I've really missed you. I didn't know how much until you called."

"Yeah, I know," he replied. He was outside, sitting at a picnic table and he said more, but the wind garbled his speech.

"What?" I asked. "Can you say that again? I lost you."

"Sorry. Gotta go."

Later that night, he sent me a text: "Out drinking with my gay friend Don. You should be here."

"Can't wait to see you," I replied.

He wrote again, at 3 a.m., quoting Simon and Garfunkel. "Kathy I'm lost I said. But I knew she was sleeping."

"You're not lost," I replied. "And I'm awake now."

I showed Todd the text.

"Are you sure you wanna do this?" he asked.

I was sure.

I counted down the days until my trip. I took a lot of long walks, and I drank more than usual. I developed a crazy idea that flying to see Jon would be something more like time travel, taking me back to my seventeenth year. I could do things differently and figure it out this time, keep him from leaving me this time, find the right thing to say. Seeing him again, I thought, would be like revisiting the ghost of my brother, reaching back through decades to reclaim someone I thought had been irrevocably lost to me. Seeing Jon would cheat death. I wanted to see his ink, and I wanted to ask him more about my younger self, and I wanted to talk and talk and talk because I had so many stories I wanted to tell him, so many things I wanted to ask, so much I wanted to know.

I wanted something else, though, but I didn't tell him this, not yet. I didn't tell anyone: I wanted to save him. I carried with me the secret, urgent belief that I alone had the power to rescue Jon because I alone shared the memory of our parallel losses. I alone understood the haunting. As I explained to Todd, I owed him my help.

A week or so before my departure, Jon stopped replying to my emails. He wouldn't take my calls.

"Why have you disappeared again?" I texted.

"Don't think I should see you," he replied. "It's dishonorable. It would disrespect your husband."

"What are you talking about?" I wrote. "He knows I'm going, he knows everything."

Jon didn't answer.

✝

Upon arrival, I walked slowly through the terminal, looking everywhere for his tall thin figure, for the shoulder-length hair that appeared in all of his Facebook photos. He hadn't answered me for two weeks, but I still refused to believe he would ghost me again, not after I came all this way. He had called *me,* after all, in the beginning. Each time I saw a tattoo, my heart clenched. I paused at the security checkpoint, and stood to the side, waiting and watching. In spite of the weeks of silence, he did have my flight information. He knew I was there. Maybe he was in the bathroom. Maybe there was traffic. Maybe he was standing off to the side somewhere watching me. I checked my cell phone again. Nothing. Baggage claim: nothing. Terminal: nothing.

I stood in a daze, looking around. I was walking through the dream that had haunted me all those months after Gerry died, chasing the shadow of someone who had already left, and I was, again, running too far behind to ever catch up. I ordered a rental car and sat in the warm parking lot for a long time, thinking. I considered plugging Jon's office address into the GPS and driving there. I knew the name of his regular bar; I could go there and hang out for the afternoon. I could buy a pack of cigarettes and sit quietly in a corner until he came in, and I could watch him for a while. I imagined the entire scene, playing it out like a high school fantasy. I knew, however, that he was gone. I felt like something profound was happening to me, something meaningful, but I couldn't figure out what. All I could think was that I'd lost something irreplaceable. Again.

I called Todd on the drive to Mickie's and told him what happened.

"Oh, sweetie. I'm so sorry. Do you want to talk?"

"No, I think I just want to sit with this for a while first. I wanted to give you the update. But thanks."

"Well, call if you need me. I'm here."

Was Jon right, that my intentions were dishonorable? Was I lying to myself about my true motives? I'll never have to confront that part of the story, or that part of myself. I'll never know what would have happened between us, what I might have said, what I might have done. Jon's absence left it all unspoken, a blankness where anything could have happened, but where nothing did. His absence became a presence, a thing, a constant fact, like the ghost pain felt by people who have lost a limb but still feel the phantom aches in the arm or the leg which no longer exists.

Four hours later, Mickie led me to her guest bedroom, with an antique bed, creamy linens scented with lavender, and a cluster of tea roses by the side table. We spent the weekend cooking and talking, sipping wine, visiting local bookstores and taking naps. On the long drive back to the airport, I kept Todd on speakerphone. He called to be sure I was okay. He thought that I'd want to talk through my visit. He relayed a message from Brian: *Mama, bring me a souvenir.*

✝

Months after that trip, I sat in my office reading back through some email from Jon, and my eyes wandered to my old copy of *Moby Dick*. I pulled the volume from its shelf and thumbed through the marked-up pages. A numbing sense of wonder overtook me as I read through my old grad school marginalia, all those scribblings about longing and desire. Back then, my Marxist advisor taught us to pay attention to currency, so I underlined each reference to money. "O men, you will yet see that — Ha! boy come back?" Ahab declares, as he sights his prey, "bad pennies come not sooner." In Melville's time, pennies were valued more highly than they are today. Bad pennies stayed in circulation because nobody was willing to take the personal loss of tossing them in the trash.

Unlucky recipients of counterfeit coins would pass them along to someone else, hoping to be done with them. But bad pennies keep coming back, drawing down the value of all other currency. I thought about Jon and his vision of life as a jar of pennies, and his cowardice, his refusal to meet me. What is the value of so many unspent coins?

Revisiting *Moby Dick*, I realized that if I read my life like a book, I can trace these layers of eerily resonant coincidence. For example: Call me Ishmael and call Jon Queequeg. Ishmael the writer befriends Queequeg, the tattooed harpoonist. New England is dark when the two first meet; it is late at night and they share an attic room at Coffin's Inn. Queequeg and Ishmael, that unlikely pair, become extraordinarily intimate friends. Together, they sign onto the *Pequod*, where they become deeply bound in an obsessive and mythical quest for something mighty, something elusive. The specter of death hovers throughout their friendship, as when Queequeg predicts his own end, and calls the carpenter to build his coffin. Ishmael, meanwhile, struggles to accept the inadequacy of his own writing, and he sees how his storytelling will always be flawed and incomplete. The images flash before me like a movie: the old trunk in the attic becomes Queequeg's coffin which then becomes Gerry's grave, covered with the mossy grass that becomes the slab rock where Richard plummeted to his death, down into the same emptiness that swallowed the *Pequod* in the end.

With *Moby Dick* as my compass, the parallel stories synchronize. Queequeg's empty coffin becomes the life-buoy that rescues Ishmael from drowning. The very emptiness of Queequeg's coffin, his absence, is what keeps Ishmael afloat. If Jon had been waiting for me at the airport, where would I be now? I look back on the wreckage and wonder.

But Jon is not Queequeg, and he's not drowned in some symbolic apocalypse, he's just gone from me. He's the friend from my youth, and our lives have gone in different directions.

✝

Forty years ago, on those mornings when I awakened to find a blank page rather than the message I desperately needed from my lost brother, I would turn to my window and stare out, haunted by his absence. If only I had known to run downstairs and say good-bye while I had the chance. If only I had known that not all of the good die young. Some of us survived.

Now, looking back through time and memory at that scared and fragile girl I used to be, I want to reach back and tell her to turn around, to turn away from the haunting. I imagine saying all the things she needs to know. She's wrong about the blank page and what it means, and she's looking for the wrong signals. Writing messages is not for the dead, it's for the living.

The dead come to us in other ways, and they call us into life.

✝

It is July 27, 2010. It's been two months since the last message I will ever hear from Jon. My family has gathered for a summer vacation reunion at an Inn on Lake Canandaigua in New York, and we are all here: Mom and Dad, Marianne, Susan, me, Paul, and James, and all of our spouses and children. Tomorrow, we celebrate my parents' fiftieth wedding anniversary. Tonight, my brothers and sisters and I have assembled for drinks at the restaurant's bar, a table at the dockside patio where we are illuminated by the setting sun. My parents have gathered most of the grandkids in their hotel room, plying them with matchbox cars, Teddy Grahams, and *Toy Story*. Here, outside, the concrete smells vaguely of beer and we joke amicably, our voices competing against the background din of outboard motors and Fleetwood Mac.

I look around the table and wonder how my life would have turned out if Gerry had never gotten sick. Would James be here? Would I be who I have become? Would I have met Todd, and would I have had Brian, and would I have developed the capacity for this tenderhearted love I feel for them? Would I have ever started writing? I look beyond the patio to the lawn where they are tossing a football, Brian bouncing with excitement on his skinny legs. Then my neck pricks as I hear it from the bar: the unforgettable trill of Billy Joel's piano. *Come out Virginia, don't let me wait...* Around the table, my brothers and sisters chatter on happily, oblivious to the change in music. What are the odds, I think to myself.

"Mama!" Brian calls from across the lawn. "Play with us!"

His hands are flapping merrily in the sunshine, beckoning me on. I go.

Notes and Thanks

Jon is a pseudonym, and certain identifying characteristics have been altered to protect his privacy; everything else is true to my memory and my research.

Early in the life of this story, I read a draft to my friends and artistic collaborators Ali Woerner and Thayer Jonutz at Take Root Dance. They transformed *Ink* into an extraordinary and beautiful two-part dance which premiered at Uferstudios/Berlin, Germany in 2015. Jon Anderson's original musical composition accompanies their performance, video excerpts of which are available for viewing on their website at takerootdance.com/videos. I'm deeply grateful for our ongoing artistic collaboration, which has been central to my own creative development.

Many friends, readers, teachers, and advisors have helped me get this far as a memoirist. I thank you all: my colleagues and students in the English Department at Oakland University; Jack Turner, Emily Bernard, Bailey McDaniel, Jessie Forton, Vanessa Stauffer, Julia McGowan, Alyce DePree, Jennifer Law Sullivan, Jennifer Heisler, Kitty Dubin, Thomas Lynch, Patricia Hampl, Bich Minh (Beth) Nguyen, Lisa Ohlen Harris, and Ethan Gilsdorf. Laura Julier, along with the anonymous readers at *Fourth Genre,* gave me very helpful feedback on an early version of this work. Fellowship support from Kresge Arts in Detroit and the Oakland University Research Office has helped along the way. I am especially thankful to, and for, the Michigan Writers Cooperative Press, particularly Kevin Avery, Melissa Grunow, and John Pahl.

I save the best for last: my family. Thanks to all the Pfeiffers, and most especially to the Estes people of my heart: Todd, Elizabeth and Brian.

MICHIGAN WRITERS COOPERATIVE PRESS would like to express our thanks to Melissa Grunow for judging the Nonfiction manuscripts this year. We are grateful for her commitment of time, and for her commitment to helping Michigan Writers Cooperative Press develop and publish new voices.

About the Judge

MELISSA GRUNOW is the author of *I Don't Belong Here: Essays* (forthcoming from New Meridian Arts Press, 2018) and *Realizing River City: A Memoir* (Tumbleweed Books, 2016), which won Second Place-Nonfiction in the 2016 Independent Author Network Book of the Year Awards and the Silver Medal in Nonfiction-Memoir from Readers' Favorite International Book Contest. Her work has appeared in *Creative Nonfiction, River Teeth, The Nervous Breakdown, Two Hawks Quarterly, New Plains Review*, and *Blue Lyra Review*, among many others. Her essays have been nominated for a Pushcart Prize and Best of the Net and listed in the Best American Essays 2016 notables. She has an MFA in creative nonfiction with distinction from National University.

About the Author

KATHLEEN PFEIFFER is an essayist, memoirist and literary critic living in Rochester Hills, Michigan. In 2012, she was named Literary Arts Fellow by Kresge Arts in Detroit. Her creative writing, which has appeared in *The Sun* magazine and the *Bear River Review*, ponders difficult situations like adultery and stepmotherhood; she also blogs at kathywrites.com. An English professor at Oakland University, Pfeiffer has numerous scholarly and critical publications, but *Ink* is her first book-length publication in a literary genre.

About Michigan Writers Cooperative Press

This book was published in the spring of 2018 in a signed edition of 100 copies.

This chapbook is part of the Cooperative Series of the Michigan Writers Small Press Project, which was launched in 2005 to give members of Michigan Writers, Inc., a new avenue to publication. Authors share the publishing costs and marketing responsibilities with Michigan Writers in return for the prestige of being published by a press that prints only carefully selected manuscripts.

Manuscripts of poetry, short stories and essays are solicited from members and adjudicated by a panel of experienced writers once every year. For more information, please visit www.michwriters. org.

Michigan Writers is an open-membership organization dedicated to providing opportunities for networking, professional growth and publication for writers of all ages and skill levels in Northwest Lower Michigan.

John Pahl, Manuscript Editor
Kevin Avery, Managing Editor
Contest Readers: Susan Odgers, Karen Stein, and Daniel Stewart
Book design by Heather Lee Shaw

OTHER TITLES AVAILABLE FROM
MICHIGAN WRITERS COOPERATIVE PRESS

The Grace of the Eye by Michael Callaghan

Trouble With Faces by Trinna Frever

Box of Echoes by Todd Mercer

Beyond the Reach of Imagination by Duncan Spratt Moran

The Grass Impossibly by Holly Wren Spaulding

The Chocolatier Speaks of his Wife by Catherine Turnbull

Dangerous Exuberance by Leigh Fairey

Point of Sand by Jaimien Delp

Hard Winter, First Thaw by Jenny Robertson

Friday Nights the Whole Town Goes to the Basketball Game by Teresa J. Scollon

Seasons for Growing by Sarah Baughman

Forking the Swift by Jennifer Sperry Steinorth

The Rest of Us by John Mauk

Kisses for Laura by Joan Schmeichel

Eat the Apple by Denise Baker

First Risings by Michael Hughes

Fathers and Sons by Bruce L. Makie

Exit Wounds by Jim Crockett

The Solid Living World by Ellen Stone

Bitter Dagaa by Robb Astor

Crime Story by Kris Kuntz

Michaela by Gabriella Burman

Supposing She Dreamed This by Gail Wallace Bozzano

Line and Hook by Kevin Griffin

And Sarah His Wife by Christina Diane Campbell

Proud Flesh by Nancy Parshall

Angel Rides a Bike by Margaret Fedder

Made in the USA
Lexington, KY
19 May 2018